Learn to Code 4 Kids with

Scratch

The Playful introduction to Coding Made Easy Guide with Projects for Young Boys and Girls

Oje Ebhota

Projects by Sesem Ebhota

Disclaimer:

Please note that the information in this document is for educational and entertainment purposes only. We have made every effort to provide complete, accurate, current, and reliable information. There are no warranties or implied. Readers acknowledge that the author is not involved in providing legal, financial, medical, or professional advice. The content of this book is taken from various sources. Before trying any of the methods described in this book, consult an authorized technician. By reading this document, the reader acknowledges that the author is not liable for any damages, direct or indirect, arising from using the information in this document, including indicative errors, omissions, or inaccuracies.

Introduction to Coding

Before learning how to code, we need to understand what coding is and what it is used for. Simply put, coding is how we let computers or any other device know what we want them to do and how to do it. So, the central concept to grasp here is, it is just an expression and a way of communicating with computers.

This is Andre. Andre is a programmer.

A programmer writes code for computer programs.

What Andre does is also called coding.

Coding means writing a set of instructions that a computer understands and then executes them step by step, as we know, computers cannot make independent decisions. However, a lot of work is being done on that. But still, we have a long way to go.

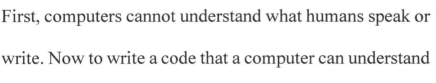

First, computers cannot understand what humans speak or write. Now to write a code that a computer can understand

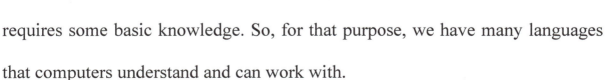

requires some basic knowledge. So, for that purpose, we have many languages that computers understand and can work with.

These languages have different rules and syntax that we must follow so that the computer can properly execute each instruction without any error.

You may be wondering why we even code, well the answer is simple. We human beings are always finding easy and more efficient ways to get our everyday jobs done. So here comes the answer, we code to automate everything we can, take any tedious task as an example.

The simplest model we can think of is a calculator. Yes, the calculator you use for complex mathematical calculations has a set of instructions stored in it. These instructions are inside a tiny computer that executes them to give accurate results. You can find millions of such examples in your surroundings. It has improved our lives in ways you cannot even imagine.

Why Learning to Code is a Good Idea

Now, you may be wondering if coding is for you. We've gone through several fantastic reasons why coding is vital to learn, not just for anybody, but particularly for kids.

There are many practical reasons why parents and teachers want their kids to learn about technology and knowing how computers function will undoubtedly offer them an advantage in life. Learning to code as a kid will prepare you for a prosperous future.

1. Problem Solving

Meet Sophia, Sophia is the head analyst at a major corporation in Silicon Valley. Sophia got her first computer as a gift from her dad when she was just 5 years

old. You can imagine how owning a computer at an early age and knowing how to use it has put Sophia in the top-earning bracket in the US. Sophia's skills are sort after by many employers, even during the pandemic when many companies were downsizing, Sophia only needed to work from home.

Computers are important. They make things like video games happen. Coding is what is used to tell computers, how they should work. That's why it is good you should learn to code as a kid, to understand how it works and use it when you grow up. The capacity to solve issues is a skill that is important in everyday life. We all want our children to be outstanding problem solvers so that they can overcome any adversity that comes their way. Learning to code allows kids to gain this sort of ability while they are still young, which can assist them later in life. It is one of the primary reasons why learning to code is essential.

2. Challenge

 Coding involves a lot of practice, sometimes you will fail to achieve what you want. When you fail, that is okay. You can learn from your mistakes. It is difficult to be successful at first, but then you will get better. These are the things that young students need to learn early in life.

When you learn to code, you earn the ability to recover from failure. You will understand that failure isn't always a terrible thing and that it may frequently be beneficial because it acts as a learning opportunity. Did you know that many innovations were discovered by accident? Yes, that is true. Sometimes, when you fail, you get to discover something else that is beneficial that you weren't looking out for. This is one of the most significant reasons why children should learn to code since they will rapidly discover that 'debugging' your code is a fun way to learn to meet challenges.

3. Enhance Logical Skill and Add Creativity

Coding is a way to teach children how to use their creativity. You need to take a vague idea and make it more specific. If the solution doesn't work, you try something else until you solve the problem.

Coding helps children develop their imagination and think in different ways. Learning to code encourages youngsters to think critically. Computer  programming is more than just learning how to enter lines of code.

It is more about educating youngsters to think in new ways. A programmer must be able to think logically to code efficiently. They must be able to identify a huge problem and break it down into smaller pieces to solve it effectively. It is known as decomposition, and it is a crucial element of computational thinking.

4. Be Independent, Be Unique

Everyone thinks differently, and view problems from different perspectives. In programming, different people come out with different ways of solving a problem, and most of the time, everyone is correct. If the distance between a cat and dog is decreasing, then there can be tons of explanations, some of which can include:

1. The cat is moving towards the dog

2. The dog is moving towards the cat

3. The Earth is shrinking due to a super-villain using a shrink ray

I could go on all my life trying to build different explanations for this, and I will still miss out on many options. Coding allows you to do all sorts of things in unique ways, and that's one of the most important things to learn when starting to code. It will bring out your creative ideas and solutions.

Coding is crucial for youngsters to learn since it encourages you to explore and gain the confidence to be creative. You will have the opportunity to create

something totally unique. Children thrive on the positive feedback they receive from producing something they enjoy. Children, like adults, require incentives while learning a language or playing an instrument. Seeing results along the road is usually enough to foster this, and this is what happens when youngsters learn

to code. Because coding is simple to learn, youngsters in particular gain confidence quickly. When kids learn to code, they gain confidence and the ability to create something entertaining and exciting.

5. Safe Future Skill

With the direction the world is headed, coding is a safe skill that will be in a lot higher demand in the future because everything is going digital. Many professions will in the future require people to have as a minimum some basic knowledge of coding.

The present way we do things have been changing for some years now and will continue to change, much of what we do will now begin to be done in the cloud. For example, now you can store your data online, shop online, play games online, social profiles, live streams, and whatnot. Many educational activities will require a minimum degree of coding knowledge. The list is endless, and it keeps increasing daily.

All of these require coding, and without coding, these would not be possible. When you consider how the world is evolving, coding is a really useful talent to have. Not only do firms in the technology industry rely on computer code, but so do many others.

A kid who learns to code will have an edge in life, with more job options accessible to them in the future, regardless of the career they choose to pursue, whether in technology, finance, retail, health, or any other. It is one of the primary reasons why kids should learn to code.

6. Learn Maths

Mathematical coding is the language of coding, and without it, there wouldn't be many things you see now. Learning to program necessitates a wide range of abilities, including data organization and analysis. Without realizing it, children improve their arithmetic abilities while coding. Math may be made more exciting and entertaining by having students, use their logic and calculating powers while producing something of their own. It is another crucial reason why coding should be taught in schools.

7. Learning How Digital Thing Works

A computer drives almost every single gadget we deal with daily in modern life. Whether it's a smartphone, a home appliance, a cash machine, or a traffic signal system as you cross the street. It is not limited to desktops, laptops, game consoles, or tablets.

A lot of effort has gone into producing solutions that are available for our use today. Learning to code will give you the chance to also be able to create solutions to our daily problems and chores. It will help you in seeing the possibilities for how coding and technology may solve future challenges.

Software is a vital component that impacts so many aspects of our life that it might be considered the world's language. Although not every profession will require coding abilities, a person who has learned the fundamentals of coding will find that the skills are transferable. It will aid them with computational thinking and knowing how digital systems work.

If you get the hang of coding, you will love it so much that you will start exploring it, and it will feel like you are playing a game in your free time to enjoy and relax.

Learning to code is a good idea if you enjoy solving basic to complex puzzles. Because we code to solve problems, the concept is similar to solving a jigsaw puzzle.

Alongside being a good idea to learn to code, it is more of an essential need for young minds. It is the age where they have a curious mind where they want to learn everything. Other than that, it has many benefits for kids. It instills the spirit of working efficiently with discipline to produce desired results.

As mentioned earlier, it is very similar to puzzles; it forces kids to concentrate and brainstorm to solve problems, which helps them in their practical life. When you have a problem to solve through coding or writing a program in any specific programming language, you start to think like a computer.

Your thinking or brainstorming style will become somewhat similar to how a computer executes instructions.

And think of a scenario when you or your parents use their computers or phones, be it a personal computer or a dedicated computer at a bus station, to book tickets. You feel very excited when you know how that computer is working, or somehow you can relate to the logic of the instructions. Almost everyone knows how to send an email, use a smartphone, play video games, but understanding the technology behind these things takes you to the next level. And

obviously, coding is behind everything, working its magic, be it day or night.

How Coding Can Impact our Lives

Coding can impact our lives and is already impacting our lives in a gazillion ways. From digital watches to watching animated movies, weather forecasts, supercomputers, even simple things like vacuum cleaners that we use in our daily lives are all because of coding.

Now consider you have a single job that you have to do a thousand times every day. With the help of coding, you can make a computer do that for you faster and more efficiently without any chance of a mistake. And you can attend to more meaningful work. It is just one example of so many others.

You can also create a game for you and your friends to start playing. Games can be single-player games or multiple-player games. The games can also be mobile, which means you can play on your phone or PC-based games that can be played on the laptop. You can also design the games to be played online, which will allow other players all over the world to be able to play the games with you. Like we have said before, whatever you can imagine, you can create with coding.

We have explored space, traveled faster than ever, transferred goods, traded, delivered products worldwide, and converted the world into a global village. We can predict diseases with the help of Artificial Intelligence, which has coding behind it. Not only has it made our lives easier, but we are also safer, sleeping peacefully because we know we have cameras and security systems installed.

Our air conditioning units that automatically maintain the temperature and other things are all functioning because of a code set. So, from above, we can conclude that in every aspect of our lives, coding is impacting our lives, making them safer and improving the quality of our lives day by day. The sound of the alarm that we wake up to, the food we order with the help of an app are all miracles of coding.

2020 will be remembered for a long time as the year the world stood still because of a pandemic that was known as Covid-19. Do you remember how you had to stay at home and could not go to school?

During that period, many countries imposed a lockdown on their citizens, so that people had to spend a lot of time at home. I bet you missed your friends during that period.

During that period, while a lot of us were watching various cartoons and playing video games, a young boy known as Kautilya katariya used his time to learn how to code and now hold the Guinness Book of Records as the youngest programmer at the age of 6.

 It doesn't matter if you are already older than Kautilya, you can still start today and become an expert in coding. As long as you know how to operate a laptop, iPad, smartphone, or gaming console, coding should not be difficult for you. So, in essence, coding is basically so well knitted in our lives and continuously adding something to our lives that we cannot think of our lives without it now.

What You Need to Be a Good Programmer

Unlike what many may suggest, there are only about three things that one needs to be a good programmer:

1. Interest

2. Logical thinking

3. Creative mind

Do you like playing games, watching cartoons and animations? In that case, you can be a programmer because programmers write code that are used to make many of the things you see or use. You are only limited by the limit of your imagination. The best way to learn to code is by starting Scratch.

Quiz Time

 Here is a quick question to see if you are a logical thinker. How many ways can you sum up other numbers to make up the number 9? Like 6+3 equals 9. If you are able to come up with more than one answer, then you are a logical thinker. There are many ways to get the number 9 from two or more other digits. We can already see that you are super intelligent, and you can be a marvelous programmer.

Creativity Test

Can you make a story about Dinosaurs, Hulk, or SpongeBob? If yes, then you have a creative mind. Everyone wants to see you make cartoons and games about these. You can use the heroes or super-villains that you have seen, or you can make new ones. With Scratch, you will be able to do this and so much more.

Now don't assume this to mean that you are already a good programmer because the attributes found in a good programmer are:

1. Willingness to learn

2. Daily coding

3. Experimenting

4. Reviewing other's code

A good programmer always wants to learn new things, this way they can be the best. So, do not be afraid to learn something new. Always keep learning new things and ways to use coding.

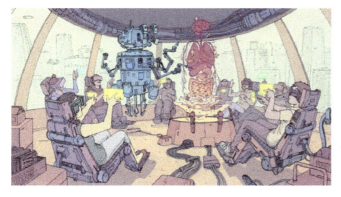 However, also make sure to write and use the code. This way, you will never forget what you learn. Moreover, practice makes a man perfect. Keep on practicing and creating whatever you want.

Don't be afraid to experiment with different tools and objects. You can always revert to undo the changes if something goes wrong. Who knows, you may come up with a trick that no one knows about. So, feel free to test out any code or tools you like.

 If you are stuck somewhere or get inspired by someone's story, game, or project, you can look at their code. Good programmers always like to know different methods of doing the same thing. So, if you want to see how a cat is flying, try to look at their code. Their code is where you will see what trick they used.

Programming Languages

Block-Based vs. Text-Based Programming

Just like we have various languages like English, German, Dutch, French, Spanish, and a host of other languages, it is the same way there are a lot of programming languages used in writing codes to control the workings of a computer.

In the programming world, many programmers use text-based programming. In text-based programming, the programmer writes his codes in the preferred programming language of a text-based screen, as if he was typing a document. There are usually no pictures or images.

Here is a list of various programming languages (code writing) in high demand:

1. Python

2. Java

3. JavaScript

4. C#

5. C++

6. C

7. Go

8. R

9. PHP

10. Swift

However, for young learners who may find these programming languages boring,

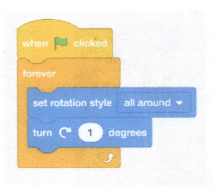

Block-based
Programming Language

using Block-based Coding may be a valuable entry point into programming. Block Coding is a method used in computer programming by converting text-based software programs into visual block formats to generate animated games, characters, and tales. Block coding allows children to learn the fundamentals and core topics using pictures rather than text-based coding.

In Block Coding, you do not have to write code, you simply drag and drop the elements, and the coding is done for you automatically.

If Block Coding programs like Scratch remove all the code writing, how does it help you learn about coding? The answer to this is that these Block Coding programs have various labels with colors and other identifiers which help beginners do a task. With or without any explanation, the user starts identifying the meaning of these statements; for example, the word "if" is used in many places and is then followed by a result.

Like many other statements used in Scratch, the 'if' statement is also used in many code writing languages. Hence, in the future, if a Scratcher is learning the 'if' statement in a text-based code writing language, then they will already know how these statements are used. The only new thing they will need to learn will be the correct way to write the statement, which is called syntax and is different in every language.

Introduction to Scratch Coding

Now that we all agree that coding for kids is a good skill to have, and we have introduced you to what is known as block-based programming, it is time to get our hands dirty and start actual programming.

I know this is the moment you have been waiting for. There are many popular block-based programming languages, but the one that stands tall among all the others is Scratch.

Scratch is an intuitive programming language created by the MIT Media Lab. It makes it easy to create interactive graphics and animations. Unlike traditional languages like Python, where programmers must write every line of code, Scratch offers colorful blocks.

It also has drag-and-drop interfaces that make for a much easier learning experience. Text-based languages like Python, Java, and C++ require you to type out your code by hand. It can make it difficult for someone who has never used these types of programming before because they will have no idea of what is going on in the program except how things are supposed to be formatted or structured overall.

Also, this formality limits its usage as people without coding experience may find themselves unable to understand these more complex languages without help from others!

This is Adora, Adora has a doll. She was gifted a doll by one of her aunties. Adora loves to play with her doll every day. Do you have a doll that you like to play with every day? But Adora's doll is just an object and does not know how to move. When the doll is placed on a table, she is not able to get it to move. One day, she decides to create a version of the doll on her computer using Scratch. She decides that the doll's name will be Dollie. What do you call your own doll?

Adora wants to create a doll that can move, dance, jump and even sing around the computer screen.

Because Adora is only just learning to use Scratch, she first has to learn the elements of Scratch.

Scratch's four main elements:

i.   The Stage

ii.   The Sprites (actors),

iii.   The Script

iv.   The Programming Palette

The elements in Scratch can be compared to a play acted on a stage because they all have similar aspects. Each element plays a role in the building process, just like how you would never find one type of actor who plays every role on an acting team.

When looking at scripts or programs, there will always be some control built into them so that it is more accessible than ever before.

Adora also likes to play video games. Sometimes she plays it on her mother's phone or the game console in the house. Through those games, she has been able to learn that every game has levels, and each level has an objective. Many of these games come with little icons called blocks that can be arranged in particular order to achieve an aim. Did you know that these coins are similar to the blocks in Scratch that are used to replace the codes used in text-based coding?

Scratch is a block-based programming language much like a virtual LEGO. Users can create programs by snapping together blocks, just as one would do with physical LEGOs! They click the green flag button in the interface to run them.

Scratch is not the only program that uses the block-based approach to create designs. There are other visual designing tools or software packages similar to those found within Adobe Photoshop or Illustrator applications.

It comes with built-in sound effects, so kids can create sounds or songs when creating their programs. All of these are done by simply moving blocks of programs on the Scratch Stage, which is where all the drama takes place like what one would do if they were snapping their own LEGO pieces together!

Scratch is REAL Coding

Scratch can be used for a lot of fun and creative kinds of stuff. Children can use Scratch to create their own interactive stories, games, and animations.

As they do this, they learn how creative thinkers should reason systematically while working collaboratively with others for a project of any kind to be made possible at all!

Scratch is a tool for learning computer programming. We frequently want kids to gain these computer-programming abilities while also developing their belief that they can learn more. To do so, it is critical to underline that Scratch is a programming language, not a game!

Things You Can Do with Scratch

With Scratch, you can program your own interactive stories and games — but it's not just for kids! Adults are also creating amazing animations with this free software. And they're sharing these creative works online in the community of other creators like them that have joined together to make projects come alive on digital tablets everywhere.

Adora *has started her Scratch coding lessons, but she wants to know what she will be able to use the Scratch to do as she learns along. Here are some of the few things that others who have learned to use Scratch just like Adora, are able to do with Scratch.*

Main Types

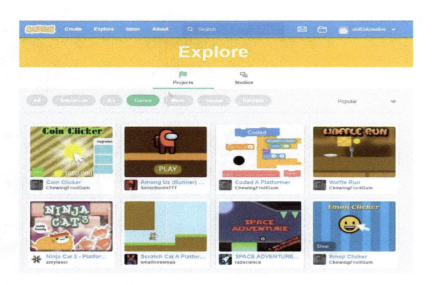

Animations

Animation is the process of trying to create a movie using characters that are not human beings. This is done by moving a character frame by frame for it to perform an act. Animations are usually incredibly difficult to create as each frame takes a lot of time to make, and the more frames you can create for each second, the smoother your animation will be. However, Scratch already has tons of characters with animations like jumping, running, flying, and more which makes it easier for you to create an animation. An example of an animation already made for you is the default cat's running or walking. You can simply alternate between the two different frames, set the gap between the frames, select a direction, and you are good to go.

If Adora wanted to create an animation of her doll jumping, she would have to create different images similar to the pictures below.

① NEUTRAL   ② ANTICIPATION   ③ JUMP   ④ MID-AIR   ⑤ FALL   ⑥ RECOVERY   ⑦ NEUTRAL

Art

Art has many types, and so is the case of art in Scratch. Most art in Scratch is interactive, which means you can do something with the art. An example of one such interactive art is where you can move to the left or right and see different art from the owner on display. So, you can also create art in Scratch and a twist or a new way to interact with it. There are even projects in the art section which let you draw and paint to make your own art.

Games

Games in Scratch are what Scratch mostly revolves around because of the amount of fun many kids derive from making games of their own. One of the most recent examples of these games is the game Among Us replicated in Scratch. Other examples are shooting, platformer, clicker, and so on. If you are interested in making games, you should definitely check out our other book on making Scratch games, as it sets the base for a bright future for any aspiring game developer. The bonus for Scratchers is that the games section gets the most views and visits.

Music

As the name suggests this should be only for projects specifically made for music. However, tons of other categories pop up in the music category because they use some kind of music like a platformer game, etc. Scratch has two related blocks to create music one is the Set instrument and the other one is the Play Note () for () Beats block to produce notes.

Stories

Do you like listening to stories? Would like to be able to also create your own stories? Scratch is a digital storytelling platform that users can use to create their own interactive stories and bring them into the classroom.

Stories in Scratch are similar to games, and the level of interaction varies. In some stories, you just press the space bar, and the story progresses whereas in some stories you have to complete certain tasks to progress. For example, Adora wants to create a story where the prince has to find the princess who disappeared and as she tries to complete the story, she will get to know the logic behind the disappearance of the princess. Some stories are like videos or animations where you click the start button or the green flag, and the whole story plays until the end.

Tutorials

Tutorials are like training that are used to teach you things about a particular topic even if they are not related to Scratch. A tutorial project can teach you how to make scrolling Backdrop in Scratch or even instruct you on how to make your own toys. So basically, tutorial projects teach you irrespective of what they are teaching.

 Adora *is so eager to get started and start exploring her Scratch coding lessons, she was even glad to know that not only is she able to use Scratch to do those things listed above, but there were also a lot more she could do.*

Here are a few more things that others who have learned to use Scratch just like Adora, are able to do with Scratch.

Other Things You Can Do with Scratch

Simulations

Simulations in Scratch are mainly two types. The first type is general, where the simulation can be used to describe a real-life or natural experience. The second types of simulation are science-based projects, typically Physics Simulations. These projects start from angles and trajectories to solar systems and explosions. The physics simulations are useful for many reasons as you can use the code present in them for your own games. For example, I want to make a game for a missile shooting game or an archer game, so now I can use the angle simulation for both of these games. Fun fact: 45 degrees is THEORETICALLY the angle for any projectile to cover the maximum distance because, in theory, we don't account for air density and other factors.

Remix

A Remix in Scratch is a project that is based on another project. After which it gets modified and distributed. Remixes may get generated from anything. Hence, there even exists projects set up specifically for others to remix (like a stage in Terraria or memes).

Operating Systems

Operating Systems like your Windows, Linux, Mac, and more cannot be completely made in Scratch but there are projects which can be called Simulations of operating systems. You can make a set of limited tasks like you would do on your own operating system. Some of these operating systems are extremely powerful, and you can do a bunch of things in them like create accounts, install apps, and more. A few examples of some outstanding operating systems are Wii v2 by SSBBM and WhiteBase OS by WhiteBase.

Programming Languages

Scratch was originally intended for people to make a lot of new things and get familiar with coding jargon like if, if-else, print, etc, without coding or manually typing. It can help you learn about other coding languages, like Java, Python, PHP, C++, and many others. So, whether it is related to Scratch programming or other coding languages, programming languages are also a part of Scratch.

Advertisements

As you can guess by the name, all types of advertisements fall under this category, whether it is of Scratch, for the poster/owner themselves, depiction of usual adverts, or adverts of some other company. In this category, you will find advertisements for Apple's iPad, Scratch Wiki, and even people making fun of the usual way advertisements are made.

Three Dimensional Projects

These are often known as 3D and are challenging to create with Scratch since the program lacks 3D capabilities. On the other hand, Scratch has produced an astonishing number of 3D projects ranging from wireframes to fully-fledged objects like a train moving in a circle. With the addition of the "run without screen refresh" custom block option, 3D rendering has become quicker.

Sprite Packs

As the name suggests, this is a project that contains many sprites or outfits. The Sprites can be from games, made with paint editors such as GIMP, or manually drawn. Some can be animated but such Sprites are rare. These are beneficial for game developers who are not extremely talented in the arts. These Sprite packs frequently have a set theme; like a user may create an "Aliens" sprite pack featuring sprites of spacecraft, planets, and aliens.

Who's That Scratcher?

Who's That Scratcher projects are games, generally part of a series, in which you use comments to guess what Scratcher is mentioned in the project. They are usually based on a well-known Scratcher. These projects gained popularity around June of 2011. They generally have a moniker that distinguishes them from others. There have been several variants.

Script Poem

A Script Poem is a narrative or message presented with all the code present in the blocks in Scratch. So, this is kind of a story that is presented using all the blocks like if, if-else, and custom blocks. The image below shows an example of how script poems work, and these are some of the easiest projects which you can make.

Petitions

Some people have started petitions in order to make things happen and urge others to remix and sign them. Examples include Stop Pollution Petition, Stop Animal

Cruelty, Stop Bullying, and more. Because of the argumentative issues they may promote, some petitions may generate a lot of heat and drama.

100% Pen

A 100% Pen project is one that employs only one Sprite as the pen. The pen is then required to draw everything, which occasionally includes the backdrop as well. 100% Pen projects might include games, drawings, simulations, and more. A couple of superb examples are confetti 100% pen and Golf-it! 100%pen.

Extensions

Extensions are scripts that may be used in other projects to enhance the capabilities of Scratch. Extensions might imitate audio effects software, such as adding a siren effect or a speaker tuning application that uses volume and pan left-right, or they can ask you to verify any changes.

Photo Dump

Photo Dumps are projects that contain a large number of photos. The photographs are generally placed here because they have nowhere else to go or because the substance of their other projects does not suit them. The project's author frequently shoots the photos. Some even make photo dumps to show off their art.

Parallax

A parallax effect is an artistic technique in which several elements of a scene or image move slowly in different directions, depending on the mouse cursor's movement and position or using any keys (arrow or W/D). You can create a parallax of a car moving by adding multiple items. Item 1 (like houses) behind the car moves faster than Item 2 (like clouds and the mountains) behind the houses. So now the car will not move but change costumes in which its wheel rotates, but the x-axis and the y-axis remain the same. However, the changing of the objects behind the car gives us the effect like the car is in motion. It is one of the ways to create a Parallax, and it is almost the same way Facebook's 3D images work.

Spam

Spam projects have no meaning or purpose, and these are the worst kind of projects like random code, images, and similar things.

Interviews

Interview projects are those in which one Scratcher questions another Scratcher. The left and right arrow keys are often used to control the questions shown on the screen.

Learning to Use Scratch Interface (UI)

 Wow!!! It looks like Adora isn't the only one interested in learning how to code with Scratch. Here is Matty. Matty is 7 years old. Matty wants to be an astronaut in the future and has been reading up about them.

He has learned that all astronauts have to have high analytical skills which is why he had been bugging his dad to get a laptop for him to start learning to code with Scratch, which is what Matty is doing right now. Matty is just getting to learn how to find his way around the Scratch interface.

The Scratch user interface is divided into several panes, set out on the left and right sides of your screen like an old-fashioned gameboard. Behind that simple-looking interface is a powerful machine capable of doing a lot of amazing things.

The interface is divided into three main sections:

i. The Stage Area is where we see our codes come alive

ii. The Block Palette is the storeroom of the blocks of codes, color-coded by categories.

iii. The Script or Coding Area is the area where the blocks from the block palette are assembled for the sprites or stage to be coded.

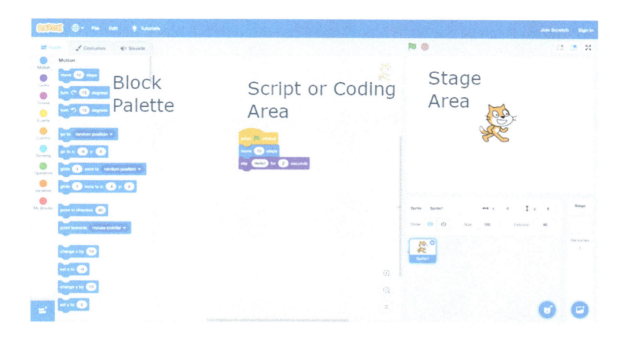

Other areas we will learn about as we go along include the Sprite Info Pane, Costume/Backdrop Pane, Sounds Pane, Toolbar, and Tutorials.

Coding with Scratch Blocks and Scripts

Scratch blocks look like puzzles, each with its own shape and slot for insertion into the stage area. These blocks are grouped into similar categories and color-coded to make it easy to find scripts more efficiently.

The blocks have different functions, which have been grouped into categories to make it easy to find them.

Now you know what modes there are, you need to know how to use the different elements present:

Block Palette: Each of the code blocks may be found in the block palette. Colors are assigned to blocks based on their categorization. Drag these blocks into the programming area to code the sprites or the scene.

Script Area: Our code is dragged to and constructed in the scripts section.

Stage Area: Here, we can view our code come to life on the stage! For instance, if we had a "when green flag clicked" event block at the beginning of our code, we may click the green flag to execute the code we wrote.

Sprite Info Pane: Here is where we may access and change information about our sprites. Click on the thumbnail of the chosen Sprite to open this window. This section also lets us remove and add different sprites.

Costume/Backdrop Pane: To access the costumes and background panes, click the center tab between the "code" and "audio" tabs. This is where we may make and modify sprites and backgrounds. Choose the relevant thumbnail in the sprite info window to move between the costume and backdrop panes.

Sounds Pane: Last option in the interface's upper left corner enables us to create and control sounds. We can even make our own!

Toolbar and Tutorials: The toolbar at the head of the screen lets us open and save projects and undo sprites deletion. By selecting the "instructions" tab, you may get various tutorials on how to accomplish almost anything in Scratch.

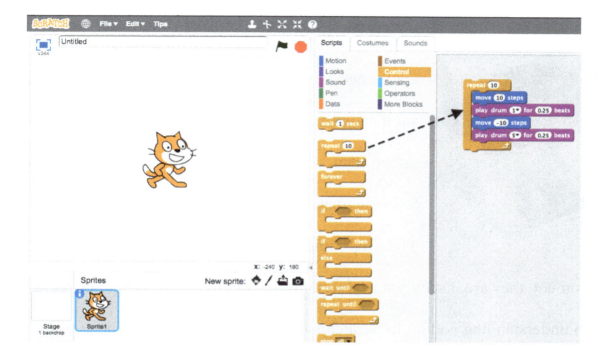

Say Hello to the Sprites in Scratch

 Sprites are characters or objects with which the user may interact. Sprites may also interact with one another, which is useful for creating an animation rather than a game. It means your Superman or Spiderman character in the project is called a Sprite.

The first time a child enters the Scratch coding environment, they are instantly introduced to the Cat, their first sprite. Sprites are vital to understanding coding in Scratch since they are what an audience sees in the front end of a game or animation.

Scratch offers a vast collection of sprites to choose from, and you're also able to make your own! So, when the cat is on stage, it's the default. Have fun experimenting with different characters till you find one suitable for the project you are creating.

Moreover, as we know Scratch is a visual drag-and-drop coding platform. It means young innovators learn the foundations of coding using visual drag-and-drop blocks (as compared to text-based coding). As a result, such sprites can take the form of forms and figures, animals, and other things.

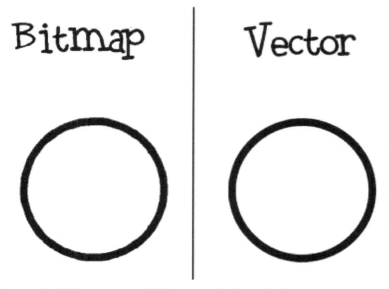

Scratch Bitmap and Vector Paint Editor

Adora and Matty now know how to insert Sprites into their projects. Sprites can be manipulated to make them do what you want. Scratch also comes with a Bitmap paint editor.

The Scratch Bitmap Paint Editor allows users to create sprites, costumes, and backdrops with the bitmap tools in Bitmap Mode. In the costume section, you have the option to customize your Sprites using the Paint editor, and if you select your Backdrop, then the same will open. When you click on costumes, the Paint editor will already be open where you can do two types of things. To know about the Paint editor more, let's talk about the Vector and Bitmap options available.

While a bitmap image contains information about the color of each pixel, a vector contains instructions about where to place each of the components. When creating a new sprite or costume, the default editor is called "Bitmap" Which can easily be converted to the vector mode by clicking Convert to Vector at any time during the design process.

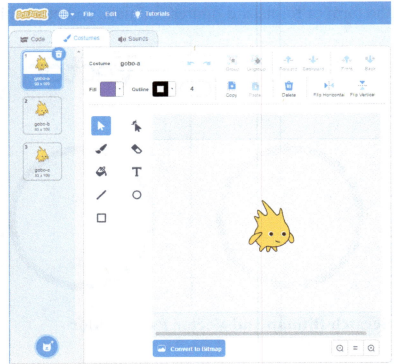

With the Scratch Vector Paint Editor, users can create sprites and backdrops in an easy-to-use vector mode. With tools like different fonts that are scalable for any size needs or shapes with adjustable colors, it is possible to make professional-looking images without sacrificing quality!

Vectors are a versatile form of graphics that can be scaled without becoming pixelated. It means you'll never have to worry about your design shrinking or growing too large for the screen, and when resized, it won't lose its quality either! To get started with Vector Mode in Scratch 2+, go ahead and select "Vector" from under Image Formats--it's really quite simple once you see how everything works together seamlessly.

Simply put, they can be differentiated as follows:

1. **Vector**: Smoother images because it can utilize shapes, curves, and lines but vector files are usually larger.
2. **Bitmap**: The image seems blurry because it consists of dots, and they seem similar to Vector if the pixels per inch are greater. Another way to put this is that each pixel's size is small.

Pixels vs. Vector

Getting Started with Scratch Blocks

Scratch coding teaches you how to make talking sprites, change costumes, expand, and shrink sprites, have sprites bounce up and down, change backdrops, and glide sprites. Hence, making coding and animating as easy as they can ever be.

Since they started learning how to code with Scratch, Matty has found himself frequently using the codes on the motion block while Adora seems to use more of the codes in the sensing blocks. But what exactly are blocks in Scratch?

To make it easy for users to understand, Scratch 3.0 decided to group similar types of codes into different color-coded blocks. Each of these blocks has different colors that make it easy for users to find the codes they are searching for when writing their programs and manipulating their Sprites. When you click any of the blocks, another menu pops up that shows the codes that the block contains. You can try it out.

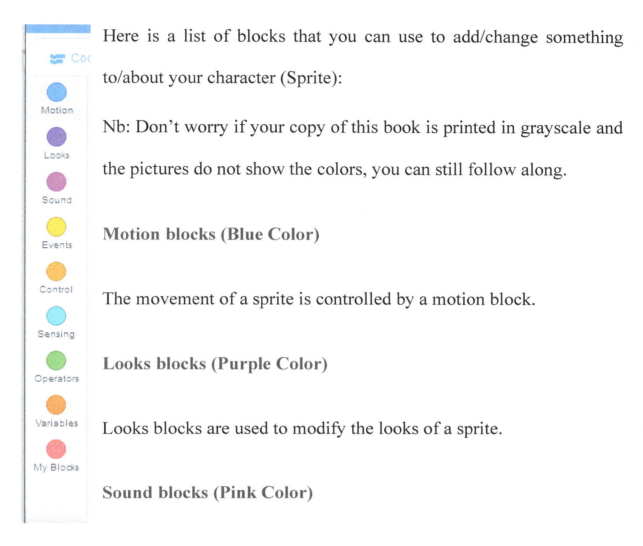

Here is a list of blocks that you can use to add/change something to/about your character (Sprite):

Nb: Don't worry if your copy of this book is printed in grayscale and the pictures do not show the colors, you can still follow along.

Motion blocks (Blue Color)

The movement of a sprite is controlled by a motion block.

Looks blocks (Purple Color)

Looks blocks are used to modify the looks of a sprite.

Sound blocks (Pink Color)

Sound blocks are used to give sprites the capacity to create sounds.

Control

All Scratch projects rely heavily on the idea of control. Under control, you'll discover code blocks that would tell your sprites how and when to move, how long they should move for, and what they should do after their duty is finished.

The majority of youngsters who try to move their character for the first time will realize that when they click the green flag, their figure may only move once instead of the ten steps they expected. We can identify a code block named "forever" under control that will give its sprite the impression of moving on its own. Sprites become stagnant and unattractive when they are not controlled properly.

Sensing Blocks

Sensing Blocks (cyan color) are kind of if-blocks where they detect any conditions. There are currently 18 Sensing blocks:

- 3 stack blocks
- 5 Boolean blocks
- 10 reporter blocks

A good example would be if I wanted to make a parallax project where a sensing block can detect the position of my mouse and move my car in the general direction of my mouse.

Operators Blocks

Operators Blocks (light green) are used for string handling and math equations. An example of string handling is:

Apples < 3

Now you can couple this with an if statement and say that if you have less than three apples, then you need to buy more. There are currently 18 Operators blocks:

- 7 Boolean blocks
- 11 Reporter blocks

Events Blocks

Event Blocks (light yellow) are used to sense events and trigger scripts. One of the most straightforward event flags is the "When green flag clicked." There are currently 8 Events blocks:

- 6 Hat blocks
- 2 Stack blocks

The Online and Offline Scratch Editor

 Matty lives in an area that doesn't always have internet connectivity. Sometimes, even when there is internet connectivity, his dad doesn't want him to get distracted with other things on the internet. So, Matty has his Scratch app installed on his computer at home, which he gets to use whether his internet is on or not.

Adora on the other hand uses the online version of Scratch. As at the time this book was written, this was known as Scratch 3.0. Adora can access her Scratch on the internet and enjoys a lot of other benefits with using this online version. She is better able to share her projects with other users all over the world as well as see other people's projects.

The Scratch app, otherwise known as the Scratch offline editor, which is the one Matty has, is a version of scratch. It can be downloaded and installed on your computer instead of using it online. In the browser-based environment (online Scratch Editor) which is the one Adora has, you have access to other people's projects and can chat with other users while working. While Matty's offline app might come in handy if teaching at home without any connectivity because then students would only need one device for educational purposes; however, this isn't always ideal considering some kids want interaction with their peers even when alone!

It is also possible teachers may wish their learners were able to participate within a supervised environment. Apart from this, both the online and offline Scratch editors have the same functionality.

Note: On mobile devices, you cannot use Scratch online (web-based). And on iOS devices, you can only use ScratchJr, which has a lot fewer features than the standard Scratch. So, if you want more functions then use a desktop.

Downloading and Installing Scratch (Windows, Mac, and Linux)

 When Matty first got his computer, he could not find Scratch on it. Initially, he was worried, but his teacher asked him not to worry, that Scratch had to first be downloaded onto the computer from the internet, and then installed before he can start using it.

Mr. Jones, who is Matty's teacher, wrote out a set of instructions for Matty to give to his dad, that will enable him to download and install Scratch on his laptop.

If you have a laptop and want to install Scratch on it, you can ask your teacher to help you if you are not able to. You can also ask your parents to help you install Scratch on your computer.

Scratch is available to download on Windows, Mac OS, Android, and Linux. Here is how to download Scratch:

1. Open the Scratch website (https://scratch.mit.edu/), or you can go to this link https://scratch.mit.edu/download and skip the next two steps

2. Scroll down to the end of the page.

3. Under the Resources tab, you will see a Download option.

4. A page will open with all the download options for different operating systems.

5. Select your operating system.

6. Click on "Direct Download" if you are using a computer; otherwise, you must go to PlayStore or Apple Store.

Note: For iOS users, you can only download ScratchJr, a stripped-down version of Scratch.

For mobile devices, after you download Scratch, there is no need to install it. The software is automatically installed. However, for desktops, you have to follow these steps:

1. Open the downloaded file.

2. A new window will open, which will ask you if you want to install Scratch. Select the option "Next."

3. Now select the folder where you want to install Scratch. You can leave the default value there otherwise you can click on "Browse" to choose a different location.

4. Click on "Next" after choosing the destination folder.

5. Now it will ask if you want Scratch to show up in the start menu (Start Menu is the Windows button on the left-bottom of your screen). Click

"Next" if you want to, or you can check the box that says, "Do not create shortcuts" and then click on "Next."

6. Now you have to wait until Scratch is installed on your computer.

7. After the installation is completed, it would be easier for you to open it if the Scratch shortcut is present on your desktop. So, make sure to check the "Make a shortcut" option and click on Finish.

That's it! Now you can use Scratch whenever you want and have fun.

Using Scratch Online

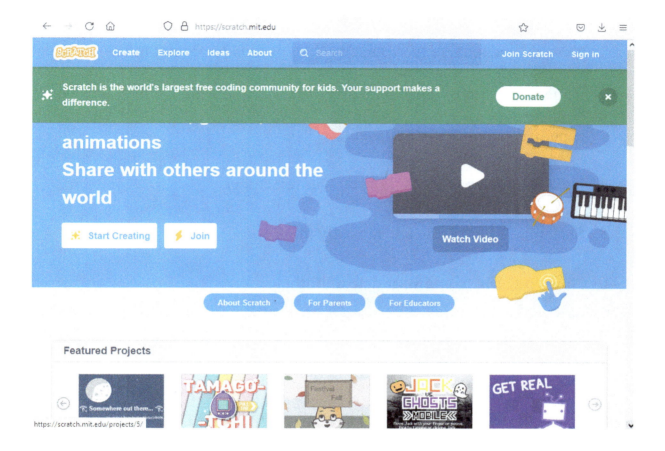

Creating a Scratch Account Online

Before Adora could start using her Scratch online, she first had to create an account. For anyone to use Scratch 3.0, the person first needs to have an account and then the person can log into that account. Since Adora was using Scratch for the first time, that was why she had to first create an account. Subsequently, she will only need to log in with the details she used when creating the account.

Here is how you can create a Scratch Account Online:

1. Go to the homepage of Scratch on https://scratch.mit.edu/.

2. On the right-upper corner, you will find a "Join Scratch" option. Click on it.

3. Now choose a name for yourself. A lot of kids prefer not to use their real names. You can try a combination of your name with that of your favorite superhero or whatever you want.

4. Now choose a password that you will remember.

5. Select the country you are currently in.

6. Now you have to add your date of birth.

7. Select your gender. You can also choose not to reveal it if you don't want to.

8. Enter your email address. It can be Gmail, Yahoo! Mail, or any other.

Yay! Now you have created your Scratch account, which will help you do wonders.

Logging into your Online Scratch Account

After creating an account with Scratch, you only have to log in on every other subsequent use. Here is how you can log in to your Scratch Account Online:

1. Go to the homepage of Scratch on https://scratch.mit.edu/.

2. On the right-upper corner, you will find a "Login" option. Click on it.

3. Enter the username you created when creating the account

4. Then, you enter the password you created when creating the account

5. Next, you click on login, then you will be taken to the home page where you can now start your project or access some of your other previous projects.

Creating Your First Scratch Project

Adora and Matty, just like you have been looking forward to this day. Matty now has Scratch installed on his computer and they have also created their Scratch accounts.

 Let's now help you, Matty, and Adora create your first Scratch project. Here is how to do it:

1. Go to the homepage of Scratch.

2. Click on the "Create" option present on the left-top corner near the Scratch logo.

A new page will open with all the different options. You have opened your first Scratch project.

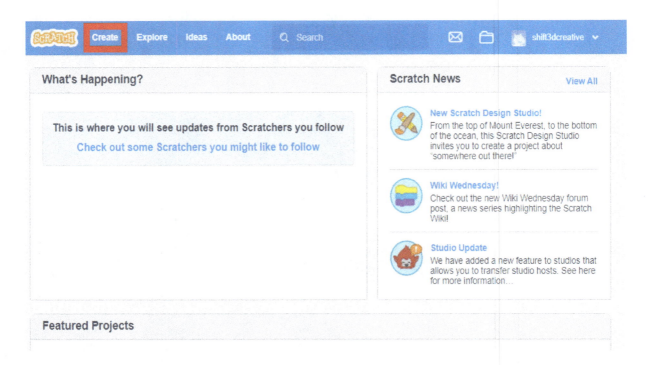

Saving your Scratch Project

Matty and Adora want to be sure they can save their projects so that they can open them later if they want to show them to their friends. There are three methods for submitting a project to the online editor, which saves your scratch project.

1. The most frequent approach to saving material is clicking the 'Save Now' button in the editor's upper right corner.

2. Another approach to saving your project is to click 'File' in the toolbar and select 'Save Now' from the drop-down menu.

3. A third approach to save your project is to use CTRL's (or CMD+S on a Mac).

Note: When the S key is pressed, the trigger is activated, and when any key is pressed, the block is activated.

When the save button displays 'project saved' and vanishes, the project has been successfully saved. A project that is being saved to the server will display 'saving project,' and a throbber (loading icon) next to the 'saving project' text.

If a project fails to save, a popup will inform the user that the project could not be saved. In the dialogue, the user can save the project again by selecting 'Try Again,' or save the project as a file by choosing 'download.'

A popup appears, indicating that an error happened during a save attempt and the alternatives available to the user.

Occasionally, projects will save themselves automatically while working.

Sharing Your Scratch Project

The remixing community of Scratch has given users the opportunity to share their projects with others who may want access or ownership. To do so, all you have to do is enable Sharing and remove any personal information from your project before releasing it.

Scratch's sharing feature provides every user around the world an open invitation and is one click away from sharing your project or accessing someone else's creative vision--whether they're friendly acquaintances or total strangers unfamiliar with what makes up YOUR studio space.

1. Log in to www.scratch.mit.edu.

2. Click the My Stuff button in the upper right corner of the web page.

3. To find out which projects have been shared, look at the information on the far right. If the project has been shared, the option to "Unshare" becomes available. The Delete option is available if a project has not been shared.

4. To share, click the project's title.

5. Select the Share option.

6. Fill out the Instructions and Notes and Credits boxes before adding one to three tags.

On the other hand, for Matty to share a project created using the Scratch Offline Editor, he has to go to the File menu and select Share to Website. Log in to your Scratch account and then proceed with Steps 2–6 above.

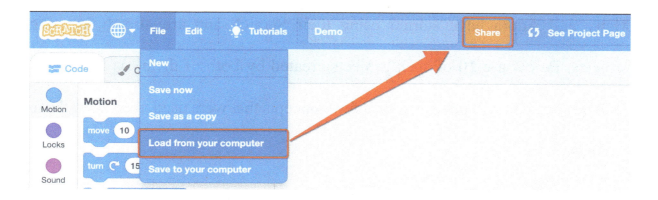

How to Add Media to Scratch

The backpack is a Scratch 3.0 project editor tool that allows users to move scripts, sounds, and costumes across projects. Drag and drop sprites, costumes, scripts, and sounds from other projects into it, then effortlessly drag and drop them into their own project. This may be used to duplicate a script or to add a script to a separate project.

Open the backpack by tapping on the "Backpack" tag present at the bottom of the screen to add media to it. Then insert a sprite, sound, costume, or script fragment. There appears to be no limit to how much media the backpack can hold. For organizing, media may also be clicked and moved around the bag. To remove media from the backpack, you have to right-click or press and hold the appropriate item and choose "delete."

Creating Scratch Projects

Matty and Adora have started using their Scratch and are already creating projects. Below are 10 of such projects created by both of them. At the end of each project, you will have learned a few concepts that were used in creating those projects.

The projects have been explained in a step-by-step manner so that you too can also create them as your own projects.

Project #1: Adding and Removing Sprites

Let us get some of the simplest kinds of stuff out of the way before we move on to bigger projects. Most projects in Scratch involve adding, manipulating, or deleting Sprites, so it is better we begin with that.

Deleting A Sprite

On Scratch, every 'New Project' should start with the Cat Sprite. Left-click on the garbage can present in the upper right corner of the Sprite you want to delete in your Sprite Pane.

Adding A Sprite

1. In the Sprite Pane, hover your mouse over the Choose a Sprite icon.

2. The magnifying glass icon should now be selected.

3. In the Sprites Pane, select the Sprite magnifying glass icon.

4. It will open the Scratch Sprite library. To locate a Sprite, you may scroll through all Sprites, use the search box, or pick a category from the top of the menu.

5. By left-clicking on the Sprite you want to code, you may add it to the list.

6. The Sprite you choose will now display on your Stage as well as in your Sprite Pane.

Great job! The sprite you selected may now be seen on the Scratch stage and in the Sprite Pane.

Creating A Sprite

You can even make a brand-new Sprite of your own. To do this, you must follow these steps:

1. In the Sprite Pane, hover your mouse over the Choose A Sprite symbol.

2. In the Sprite Pane, select a Sprite icon.

3. Choose the paintbrush icon.

4. It will lead you to the section where you can start making your own sprite using the tools provided to you.

Practice Exercise 1

1. Add two Sprites: A building and a flying cat.

2. Without deleting, hide the building.

3. Unhide the building and make the flying cat larger than the building,

4. Make the cat smaller and the building larger.

Project #2: Adding a Background

Scratch comes with various backgrounds and backdrops that you can use to replace the default one.

Here is how you can add a backdrop to your scene:

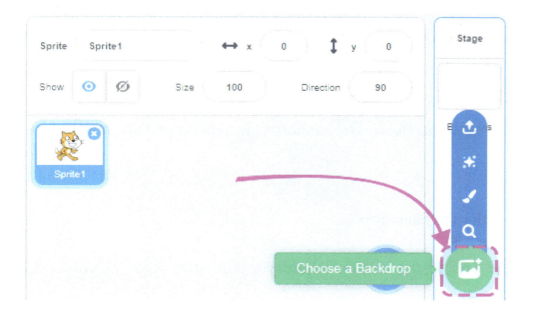

1. In the lower right corner of your screen, hover over the Choose a Backdrop symbol as indicated in the picture above.

2. Click the button to open the Scratch Backdrop library. To locate a Backdrop, you may scroll through all of them, use the search box, or pick a category from the top of the menu.

3. Choose the Backdrop that you want to utilize on your Stage.

4. Now the Backdrop will appear on your Stage as well as in your Backdrop menu. You may need to wait for a few minutes for it to show up.

Later on, you will learn how you can change Backdrops in the operator's category (Purple section) with the code "Switch backdrop to NAME" as you run the program.

If you prefer and believe you have an artistic mind, you can also design your own Backdrop from scratch. To do this, you should do the following:

1. In the lower right corner of your screen, hover over the Choose a Backdrop symbol.

2. Choose the paintbrush icon. The paintbrush icon is the one that has the look of a brush.

3. Option to color the backdrop.

4. It will take you to the section where you can start creating your own Backdrop using the tools provided.

5. Paint the background area.

6. This Backdrop will display on your Stage as well as in your Backdrop menu.

Backdrop Changes

1. Select a sprite and two or more backgrounds for your project that you wish to write to activate the Stage. Matty chose the Rocketship sprite, Star's background, and Moon backdrop for this project.

Rocketship

2. Once you've decided on your two backgrounds, click on the backdrop image below the Stage to the right of your Code Area. You will be able to code your background because of this.

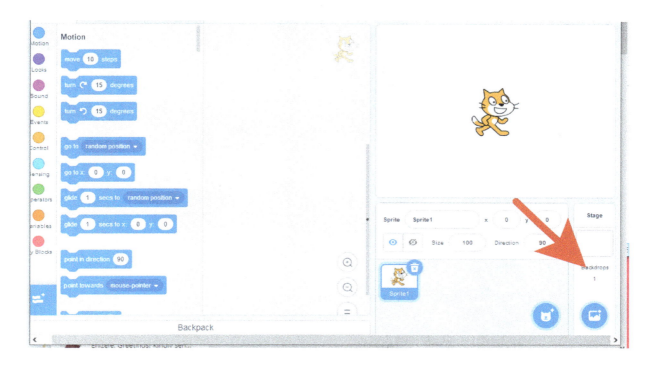

3. Check to see if the two backgrounds you choose are still available for usage. To do so, click on Backdrops, which is located right over the Block Palette to the left of your Code Area.

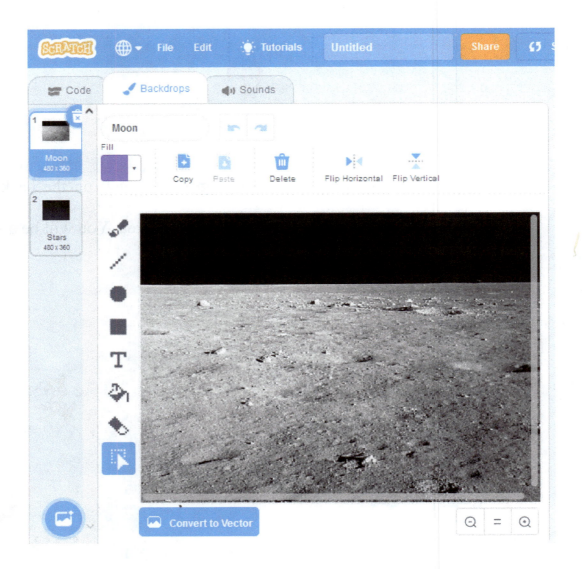

4. In the backdrops Paint Editor, you'll see all your selected backgrounds on the left of your screen.

5. Ensure you have selected the code button beside the backdrop button at the top of the block area. Drag the "when green flag clicked" block from the Block Palette's Events category into your Code Area. It instructs your code to be executed when the green flag just above Stage is pressed and when the block itself in Code Area is clicked.

6. Drag a "switch backdrop to..." block from the Block Palette's Looks category onto your Code Area. Connect this block to the "when the green flag is clicked" block.

7. Every time use the drop-down option to pick whatever background you want your game/story to begin with.

8. Drag a "wait 1-second" block from the Block Palette's Control category onto your Code Area. Connect this block to the "change backdrop to..." block.

9. You may alter the number within the white bubble by clicking on it and entering the desired number of seconds. Matty set the seconds to three for this project. This is because he wants the Stars' background to show for three seconds before switching to the moon backdrop.

10. Drag another "switch backdrop to..." block from the Block Palette's Looks category into your Code Area.

11. Select the backdrop you wish your code to change to from the first background and wait for the block using the drop-down option. Matty chose the Moon background as the second backdrop in this code for this project.

12. Run your code! Select the green flag there at the top of your Stage or the green flag block present in your Code Area.

Can you recount a tale or an event using the sprite and two backdrops?

In this episode, for example, Matty decided to present a narrative about the first-time mankind landed on the moon! He wasn't sure if he should offer information by programming the Rocketship to speak, or he should add an additional sprite that utilizes either the recorded voice or speech bubble options to tell us all about the initial landing!

To test your project, click the green flag at the top of the stage area, and watch your project run. On Scratch 3.0, you can also use the see project page to run the project.

Were you able to successfully recreate this project?

_____

What lessons did you learn from this project?

_____

Did you have to adjust some sections of the instruction to make it work?

_____

If yes, what did you change or add to make this project work for you?

_____

Practice Exercises 2

1. Use the Concert background.

2. Duplicate the Concert background.

3. Flip the Concert background.

4. Use the appropriate code blocks to keep changing between the backgrounds forever,

Project #3: Make Sprite Say Something

Make Your Sprite Say Something or Make a Noise

Now we expect that you have already added your Sprite and Backdrop. But this time, I want you to take your Sprite to the Jungle. A small hint would be that the Jungle Backdrop is already available! Now let's make your Sprite say something. Adora decided to use her cat and make it say "Hello" when it Meows. Here's how you can do it:

1. To begin, ensure that your sprite gets highlighted inside the Sprite Pane. It is highlighted when you select it.

2. Now drag a "When Green Flag Clicked" block from the Event's category of the Block Palette into the Code Area. This block will instruct your code to run when you click on the green flag above the stage. Every piece of code you write for your sprite must start with an Events block.

3. Then, under the Blocks Palette, navigate to the Looks category. This category contains blocks that will alter the appearance of your sprite.

4. Choose the "Hello for 2 Seconds" block. Drag this block onto the Code Area and position it beneath the 'When Green Flag Is Clicked' block.

5. Click on the Hello and type in Meow!

To modify what appears in the Stage's speech bubble, click on the white input box that reads "Hello" in the Code Area and write whatever you want your Sprite to say. Adora changed hers to "Meow!" You may alter the number of seconds the speech appears on Stage by clicking on the white input box with the number "2." Adora set her own to one second so that the speech bubble stays on the Stage long enough to be read. Now when she joins the Meow and says Hello code, our cat meows and says hello! How cool is that!?

To make your sprite speak more, add one "Say Hello for 2 Sec" block to the Code Area and place it beneath your script! You are free to use as many "Say" blocks as you want! The dialog boxes will play in the sequence you specify in the script, thus the cat sprite would first say "Let's Play Hide and Seek" for four seconds, followed by "Can I hide first?" for four seconds in another speech bubble.

If your Sprite has a lot to say, it's a good idea to utilize more than one "Say Hello for 2 Seconds" block. It will break up your speech and keep your speech bubbles from becoming too lengthy. We typically pause and take breaths after our phrases when we talk, so by splitting your Sprite's sentences into distinct speech bubbles, you may achieve the same effect with its speech.

To test your project, click the green flag at the top of the stage area, and watch your project run. On Scratch 3.0, you can also use the see project page to run the project.

Were you able to successfully recreate this project?

_____

What lessons did you learn from this project?

_____

Did you have to adjust some sections of the instruction to make it work?

_____

If yes, what did you change or add to make this project work for you?

_____

Practice Exercises 3

1. Make your cat say your name.

2. Make your cat say something funny.

Project #4: Customizing Sprite Costumes

Add Your Sprite and Background

Matty is really beginning to enjoy programming and has decided to undertake a very special project. He wants to create a project that will change the way the Sprites he puts on the screen change its outlook or costume while still on the screen.

To do this, he was careful enough to select a sprite that has more than one costume. A costume is a slightly different version of the same Sprite image. Some of these in the Scratch collection have a single costume, whereas some have several. To determine if a Sprite has several costumes, proceed to the sprite's library, and put your cursor over it until a blue outline forms encompassing it. If the Sprite has more than one outfit, it will switch between them.

Change the costume of your Sprite by coding it.

Matty planned to make an animation of a Sprite by rotating its outfits. He is using the Dragon sprite because it has more than one costume and can exhale fire.

The first Dragon costume is the default outfit that will arrive in the Sprites Pane, where the cat is.

Dragon-b is a little different, with curved legs and an extended neck to give the impression that it is flying. Dragon-c is engulfed in flames.

To know if a Sprite has more than one costume, just hover your mouse on that Sprite, if it changes into more than one shape when your mouse is above it then that Sprite has a costume. You can play around with that to see for yourself.

1. To begin, he started by placing an Events block in the Code Area that says, "when this sprite clicked."

2. By now, Matty knows that to change the costume of the selected Sprite, he has to start coding it.

3. In the Blocks Palette, he selected the Controls category. These are the blocks that govern our scripts, such as the number of repetitions our code runs or how long the blocks in our script will pause before executing. You can drag a "wait 1 second" block into the Code Area and place it beneath the "switch costume to" block.

4. By clicking on the white input bubble, you may alter the amount of time it takes for the Sprite to shift from one outfit to the next. Matty has set the seconds to 0.25sec for this episode. This allows the costumes to change faster and appear smoother than if he had a one-second delay time.

5. Under the "wait 0.25 second" block, you can add an extra "switch costume to" block from the Looks section just like Matty did.

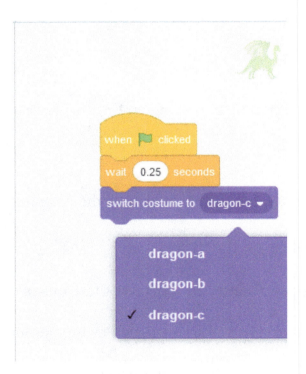

6. Pick a different costume from your initial Looks section by using the drop-down list on the "switch costume to" block. He is turning into a dragon-a costume.

7. Matty has now added a wait block beneath the other "switch costume to" block. Keep in mind the input value on this block matches the value of the

very first wait block. Just like you see in the image below, each of the wait blocks has a numeric value of 0.25.

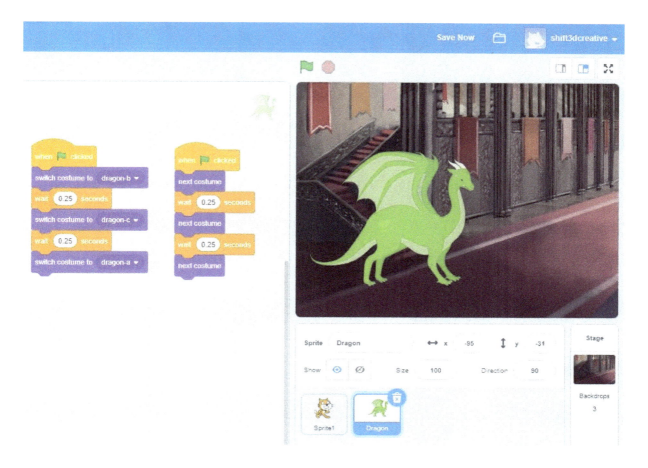

Hurray, the animation is now ready, and it is time for Matty to put his code to the test! If you have followed the steps Matty followed, you too can select your Sprite to see its outfits change. If you also successfully did this, then just like Matty, you have just successfully created an animated sprite! Experiment with various Sprites and inputs to observe how the movements of your Sprite vary.

You can also customize your Sprites and add your own finishing touches. Simply select the Sprite and go to the costume option. From there you can start painting!

To test your project, click the green flag at the top of the stage area, and watch your project run. On Scratch 3.0, you can also use the see project page to run the project.

Were you able to successfully recreate this project?

_____

What lessons did you learn from this project?

_____

Did you have to adjust some sections of the instruction to make it work?

_____

If yes, what did you change or add to make this project work for you?

_____

Practice Exercises 4

1. Give the cat a mustache!

Project #5: Make Your Sprite Take a Walk

It is time for Matty and Adora to take their projects further. They now want to make their Sprite walk across the screen. Adora wants to make her doll Sprite jump up and down the screen. For the Sprites to move across the screen, they have to learn about the X-coordinate, Adora understands that the Y-coordinate is very important if she wants her Sprite to be able to jump up and down the screen. So, what do we mean by the X and Y coordinates?

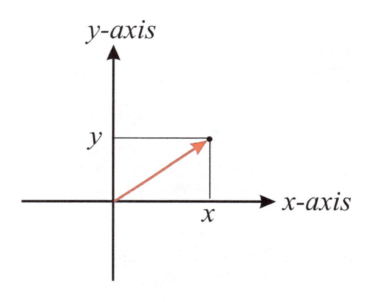

X-coordinate

The X-coordinate of a sprite is its position on the Stage's x-axis (horizontal). The number changes based on how far to the right or left the Sprite is on the Stage, where the center is 0.

Y-coordinate

The Y-coordinate of a sprite is its position on the Stage's y-axis (vertical). Value increases or decreases based on how considerably up or down the Sprite's location is from the center on the y-axis.

With that out of the way, let us join Matty and Adora to work on their project. Be sure to follow the instructions below. Once you have mastered them. Try to do them on your own without referring to the instructions and see if you can do them on your own. Who knows, you may even come up with something better than that of Adora and Matty.

Gliding from One Point to Another

1. Each time you execute your code, select, and drag the Sprite on the Stage to where you require your Sprite to start.

2. It will alter the x and y coordinates of the Sprite. Drag a 'when this sprite clicked' block from the Block Palette's yellow Events category onto the Code Area. When you click on your Sprite on the Stage, this block will instruct your code to run.

3. Use the 'go to x: y:' orders block from the Block Palette's Motion category onto the Code Area. When you execute your code, its block will inform Sprite where to start on the Stage. The y-coordinate and x-coordinate inside the block correspond to the y-coordinate and x-coordinate of your Sprite.

4. Drag a 'wait 1 second' block from the Block Palette's Control category onto the Code Area. This "wait" block instructs your Sprite to wait a specified number of seconds before gliding to the next provided x- and y-coordinates. In the white bubble on the block, you may alter the number of seconds.

5. Drag your Sprite to the next place on the Stage by clicking and dragging it. I dragged my Sprite to the bottom of the ladder in the image below.

6. It will alter the y and x coordinates of the Sprite in the Sprites Pane.

7. Use a 'glide 1 sec to x: y:' coordinate block from the Block Palette's Motion category onto the Code Area. This block instructs your Sprite to glide for 1 second to the new x- and y-coordinates. This block will hold the x-coordinate and y-coordinate from the previous step.

8. Click on your Sprite on Stage to test your code!

To test your project, click the green flag at the top of the stage area, and watch your project run. On Scratch 3.0, you can also use the see project page to run the project.

Were you able to successfully recreate this project?

_____

What lessons did you learn from this project?

_____

Did you have to adjust some sections of the instruction to make it work?

_____

If yes, what did you change or add to make this project work for you?

_____

Using X and Y Coordinates to Locate your Sprite on the Stage

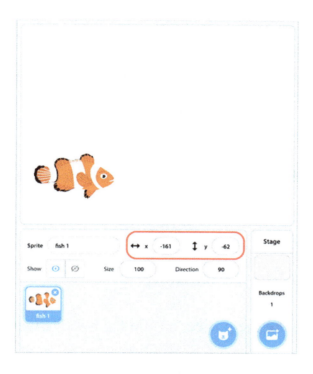

1. Before we begin coding, click, and drag your sprite to the right on the stage. Take note of how the value of the x-coordinate in the Sprites Pane increases! Examine how the x-coordinate change as you move the sprite around.

2. Now, drag your sprite to the left and note how the x-coordinate value in the Sprites Pane decreases. Take note of how the value of x shifts again.

3. When you drag the sprite up and down the stage, the value of the y-coordinate in the Sprites Pane increases. Take note of how the Y-coordinate changes in value.

4. Moving the sprite downward reduces the value of the y-coordinate in the Sprites Pane.

What lessons did you learn from this exercise?

_____

Did you have to adjust some sections of the instruction to make it work?

_____

If yes, what did you change or add to make this project work for you?

_____

Set Your Sprite's Start Position

Matty has decided to take the project a little further. He wants to make the Sprite move. He has to plan the movement path of the Sprite by deciding where the starting point will be, where the Sprite will move to, and where he wants it to end up in.

1. Use a "when green flag clicked" block from the Block Palette's Events section into the Code Area.

2. Put your Sprite in the Stage area where you need your Sprite to start every time you execute your code. It will alter the y and x coordinates of the Sprite in the Sprites Pane.

3. Use a "go to x: y" orders block from the Blocks Palette's Motion section onto the Code Area. This Motion block's default x-coordinate and y-coordinate input bubbles will be set to the precise location of your Sprite on the Stage (which means that it will have the same coordinates that are

set in the Sprites Pane). When you press the Green Flag, this block will direct your Sprite to that place.

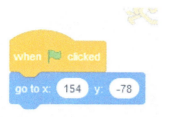

Shifting Left and Right

1. Matty started a new script that will help our Sprite move left and right. Use a "when space key pressed" piece from the Block Palette's Events category into the Code Area.

2. This implies that any code he writes below this new Events block will execute when you press the spacebar, rather than when you press the Green Flag as the old script did.

3. Select the "right arrow" from the drop-down option to the "when space key pressed" code. The code written beneath this keyboard input Events block will only be executed when you hit the right arrow key on your keyboard.

4. Select the "change x by" section from the dark blue Motion section in the Blocks Palette. Drag this piece onto the Code Area and position it beneath the "when right arrow is pushed" Events section. The "change x by 20" block instructs your Sprite to travel down the x-axis, since the figure is rising by 20, implying that the Sprite is being moved to a bigger x-

coordinate. Because we've linked this Motion block to the right arrow keyboard input, pressing the right key will cause your Sprite to travel twenty steps to the right.

5. Now we'll use identical methods to have the sprite travel to the left. Drag another "when space key is hit" section from the Block Palette's Events section into the Code Area.

6. Select "left arrow" from the drop-down option in the "when space key pressed" block. Now, the code you put beneath this Events block will only be executed when you hit the left arrow key on your keyboard.

7. Select another "change x by" section from the dark blue Motion section in the Blocks Palette. Drag this block to the Code Area and place it beneath the "when left arrow is pushed" Events block.

8. To shift the Sprite to the left, we need to alter the "change x by 10" Motion block. Adjust the number in the white input bubble on the duplicated "change x by 10" block to -10. This instructs your Sprite to travel to the left along the x-axis when the number decreases. When you hit the left arrow key on your keyboard, your Sprite will now travel ten steps to the left along the x-axis to a new, smaller x-coordinate.

9. The Code Area will now contain three Event pieces with code underneath each one.

10. Run your code! Click the Green Flag, then use your keyboard's left and right arrows to move the Sprite left and right!

Setting Your Sprite's Start Position

1. Use a "when green flag clicked" block from the Block Palette's Events section in the Code Area.

2. Put your Sprite in the Stage area where you need your Sprite to start every time you execute your code. It will alter the y and x coordinates of the Sprite in the Sprites Pane.

3. Use a "go to x: y" orders block from the Blocks Palette's Motion section onto the Code Area. This Motion block's default x-coordinate and y-coordinate input bubbles will be set to the precise location of your Sprite on the Stage (which means that it will have the same coordinates that are set in the Sprites Pane). When you press the Green Flag, this block will direct your Sprite to that place.

Moving Up and Down

1. Use a "when space key is pushed" piece from the Block Palette's Events section.

2. Select the "up arrow" from the drop-down option in the "when space key pressed" section. This tells your Sprite that pressing the up arrow will execute the code below it.

3. In the Block Palette, use the "change y by 20" piece from the Motion section. Connect this piece to the 'when the up-arrow key is pressed' piece. This "change y by 20" element instructs your Sprite to advance on the y-axis as the amount grows larger. When you hit the up button on your keyboard, your Sprite should travel twenty positions up to a new y-coordinate on the y-axis.

4. Select the "down arrow" from the drop-down option in the "when space key pressed" piece. This tells your Sprite that pressing the down arrow will execute the code below it.

5. In the Block Palette, use a "change y by 20" piece from the Motion section. Connect this piece to the "when the down arrow key is pressed" piece.

6. Change the number to -20 by clicking on the white bubble inside the "change y by 20" box. This instructs the Sprite to travel down the y-axis as the amount decreases. If you hit the down button on your keyboard, the Sprite should shift twenty positions down to a new y-coordinate on the y-axis.

7. Run the code, which you can do so by hitting the green flag button at the top of your Stage.

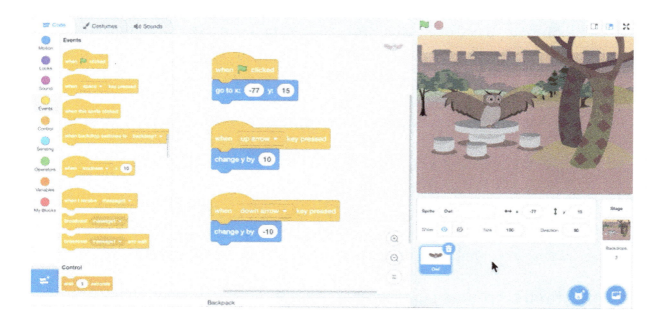

Flying

Now, let us see how we can help Matty fly the Sprite.

1. In the Sprite Pane, click on the Sprite to make it ready to accept code.

2. Use a "when space key is hit" block from the Block Palette's Events category in the Code Area. When you push the spacebar on your keyboard, this yellow Events block will inform your code to run.

3. You may select a different key on your keyboard as the input for starting your code by clicking the drop-down option on this block. You can select a letter, a number, or an arrow key.

4. In the Blocks Palette, navigate to the dark blue Motion category. This category contains blocks that control the movement of your Sprite in various ways. Choose the "glide 1 sec to random place" option. Drag this

block onto the Code Area and place it beneath the "when space key is pressed" block.

5. This Motion block will cause your Sprite to glide to a random place on the Stage, taking one second to arrive.

To run your code, use the space bar on your keyboard! When you press the spacebar, you'll see that the Sprite glides to a random location on the Stage in one second! If you keep hitting the spacebar, your Sprite will move in a new direction every second.

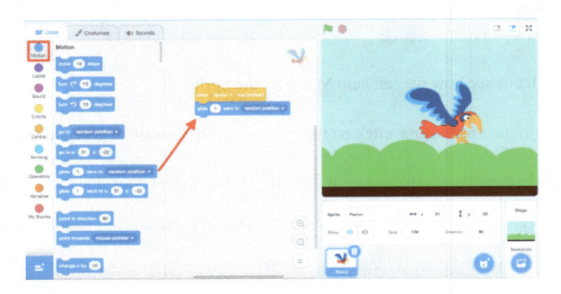

Changing the Speed at Which Your Sprite Glides

The first white space on this block is a numeric input. Here you may specify how long you want your Sprite to glide. If you increase this value, the Sprite will glide more slowly. If you reduce this value, the Sprite will glide faster.

Glide your Sprite towards the mouse pointer.

The second space on this block is a drop-down menu from which you can select the direction in which the Sprite will glide. You may adjust the direction of the sprite by clicking on this option, which will cause it to glide towards the mouse cursor instead of a random place.

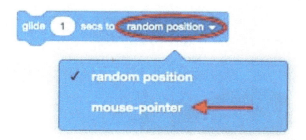

How to Make a Ball Bounce in Scratch

Remove Scratch Mascot and replace it with Ball Sprite

We won't need to have the default Sprite, so erase it by clicking the trash-can symbol to the right of the Sprite or below the canvas. Alternatively, we'll go to the Library and pick the first ball.

Allow the Ball to Bounce

We all know that a ball may bounce in a variety of ways, just like in most games. When it is dumped on the ground, hurled against a wall, smacked with a racket, slapped, kicked, and so on. Aside from a bowling or wrecking ball, we understand that there are other methods for physically making the ball bounce. One question still stands, however, at what point in the game do we want to see our ball bounce?

The same is true here. So, let's start the event with "when this sprite clicked," and then we'll determine the farthest position on the right/left side of the screen and have the ball bounce back and forth to simulate a bounce. And with that, our ball will come to life a bit more. All that remains is to investigate a couple of additional ways we can program our ball to bounce. So far, we've made our Ball Sprite go from one side of the screen to the other. Even though it appears to be bouncing, it is only doing so from left to right.

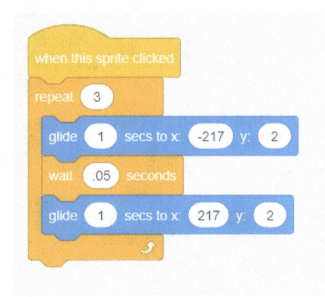

Make the ball bounce off all four "walls" by customizing it.

What about if we wanted to witness our ball bounce against the canvas's edges? Fortunately, Scratch provides an easy solution for this, so all that remains is to apply logic. Scratch, for example, already contains a block that we can utilize to make it bouncy. It's even written for us: "if on edge, bounce." So, don't delay and put it to use.

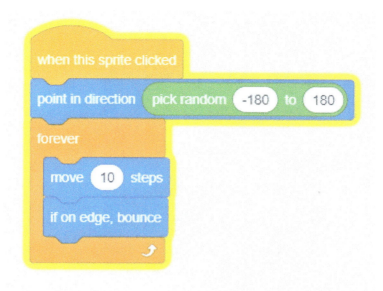

Make the ball bounce off another Sprite by Customizing it.

What if there is another Sprite in the very same simulation, and the ball is expected to ricochet off that Sprite as well, to make the experience more realistic?

It is also a simple task. Bring out the Cat, a fake sprite with no function, to serve as a steppingstone (or, in our case, "bouncing stone").

But before that, keep in mind that we'd have to apply some kind of precondition to make it happen. Before we go into the blocks, let's approach it this way: "If the ball collides with Cat, then what?" What about adjusting the route in the opposite direction of the Ball/Sprite collision? As a result, the phrase "a 180-degree turn" got coined.

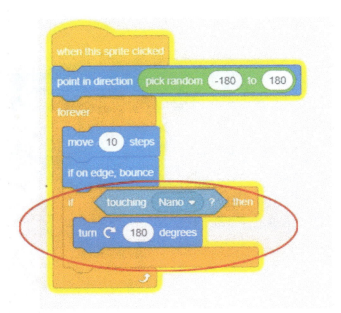

Those were a lot of mini-projects in 1 project. Do not worry if you were not able to get all of them at once, you can always come back to try again.

To test your project, click the green flag at the top of the stage area, and watch your project run. On Scratch 3.0, you can also use the see project page to run the project.

If you were able to get up to this point, then you deserve to give yourself a high five.

Were you able to successfully recreate this project?

_____

What lessons did you learn from this project?

_____

Did you have to adjust some sections of the instruction to make it work?

_____

If yes, what did you change or add to make this project work for you?

_____

Practice Exercises 5

1. Make your cat move from one backdrop (room/place) to another.

2. Make a bird fly forward.

3. Make your ball bounce off the four walls and your Sprites.

4. Now make your cat and ball bounce off each other.

Project #6: Conditional Statements

Matty and Adora are so excited about the projects they have been able to create. They have tried their hands on a lot of things and are very happy with the progress they have made.

Their teachers and parents are also very happy with them. Adora and Matty have decided to take up new challenges, they have decided to learn about conditional statements.

What are conditional statements in coding?

A Conditional Program is a program that contains conditional statements, and the technique is known as Conditional Programming. Conditional

statements determine whether a Boolean condition supplied by the programmer is false or true.

They allow you to test a variable that you set against a value. Or you can also compare a variable to a different variable and have the computer respond a certain way if it is satisfied and another if it is not. It makes any coding language extremely strong and allows it to be utilized for a wide range of tasks, from constructing basic calculators to commanding robots.

A great example of this is the working of a light bulb. If a light bulb isn't functioning or turning on, you should investigate if the switch is turned on or off before anything else. If the switch is turned off, then you flip the switch. However, if it is already on but the bulb is not turning on, you repair or change and if you can, then check the connection. You respond to the circumstance or condition.

Before we go any further, let's look at several key operators that produce Boolean results and serve as conditional statements. The following is a list of operators and their functions:

IF X < Number

The block determines if the number or value of a variable X is smaller than the number used for comparison. If it is less than that, the block returns true; otherwise, it returns false. This block also works with letters and numbers. Letters near the beginning of the alphabet (e.g., x, y, z) are worthless in Scratch than letters at the end (e.g., a, b, c).

IF X = Number

Then block determines if the variable X and number used for comparison are the same or equal. If the values are the same, the block returns true; otherwise, it returns false. Here it does not matter if you input capital or small letters.

IF X > Number

The block determines whether the variable X is higher than the corresponding number. If the following number is smaller than the first, the block returns true; otherwise, it shows false.

AND Operator

This block connects a couple of Boolean blocks, thus both must be true for the block to be true. If and only if both conditions are true, then the block returns true; otherwise, it returns false if even one of them is false or both are false.

Or Operator

This block also connects Boolean blocks in pairs so that either one of these can be true in order for the block to return true. As long as one of them is true, the block will be true. If neither of the conditions is true, then the block returns false.

Not Operator

If the Boolean within the block is false, the block will be true; if the condition is true, the block will be false.

Conditional Blocks

A total of 5 conditional blocks in Scratch are listed below:

Repeat: Any blocks included within the Repeat block will loop a specified number of moments before letting the script proceed. All numbers you input here will get rounded off.

Forever: Any blocks stored within the Forever block will loop a specified number of times, similar to the Repeat and Repeat Until blocks. Adora and Matty have been told that this block will continue to loop forever except when the red button gets clicked, the Stop All block is activated, or the stop script block is activated within the loop. Because of the infinite loop, there is no bump at the bottom of the block; adding a bump would be worthless because the blocks below it will never be triggered.

If-Then: The block will do a Boolean condition check. If the condition is met, the blocks included within it will execute, and the script involved will proceed. If the condition is false, the code within the block is disregarded and the script continues (unlike the If X Then, Else block). The condition is only tested once; if it becomes false while the script inside the block is executing, it will continue to execute until it completes.

If-Else: The block will verify its Boolean condition: if it is true, the code contained inside the first place under IF (space) will be activated, and the script will proceed; if it is false, then the code included within the second code will be activated (unlike the If () Then block).

Repeat Until: This block's code will loop until the provided Boolean statement is true, after the input X condition, the code behind the block (if any) will be executed.

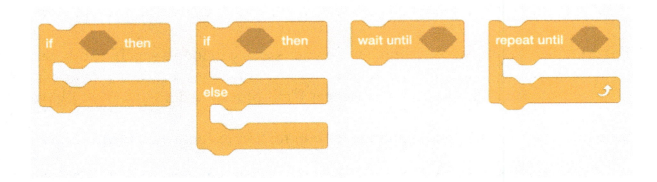

Up and Down Arrow

A recurring up-and-down motion cycle drives the bouncing animation. For instance, the arrow goes down for some time before changing direction to move up for the same time that it traveled down. The timings must be equal so that the arrow does not move upward or downward.

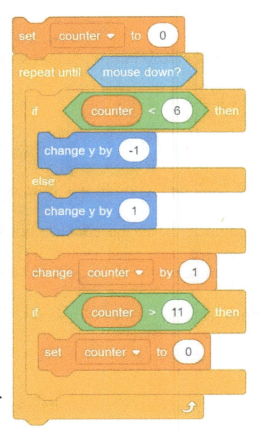

This implies we'd need some type of counter variable to keep records of how

98

often or how far the arrow has gone down, and then flip the arrow's movement so that it cycles in the same location.

Try to develop the method I'll describe below as an exercise (hint: you'll need to add a "counter" variable in the "Variables" category). Join Adora as she tries her hands on this new project, for this one, she wants to make the arrow travel down 5 steps and then up 5 steps for a total animation length of 10 steps. Here is how she achieved that.

1. Add the counter block to the script area under the if block

2. Set the counter to zero.

3. Continue until the mouse is clicked:

4. Check to see whether the counter is less than or equal to 5:

5. If this is the case, shift the arrow down by one.

6. Check to see whether the counter is more than 5:

7. If this is the case, shift the arrow up by one.

8. Add one to the counter.

9. Check to see whether the counter is more than or equal to 10:

10. If this is the case, reset the counter to 0.

In other words, this is how your code will work:

Check to see whether the counter is less than or equal to 5. (less than or equal to)

Check to see whether the counter is less than 6.

Similarly, to determine when to reset the counter, use the following formula:

Check to see whether the counter is more than or equal to 10. (greater than or equal to)

Check to see whether the counter is larger than 11.

Instead of greater than and less than, use modulo (optional alternative)

The approach used by Adora above isn't the only way to achieve the aim of cycling and bouncing arrows. While "greater than" and "less than" comparisons work properly, you can alternatively achieve the same result by using the modulo operator. The modulo operator, represented by "%" or "mod" where a "+" would typically be, returns the remainder of dividing one integer by another: For example, 6 mod 3 = 0 since 6 divided by 3 = 2 with no remainder; and 13 mod 4 = 1 because 13 divided by 4 = 3 with a remainder of 1

Modulo is a handy operator since it returns 0 for all divisor multiples. In the above example, 6 mod 3 = 0, however, every multiple of 3 is likewise 0. We can utilize this characteristic to create a condition in which the direction of movement changes every time "counter mod n = 0," where n is half the duration of the whole cycle (e.g., 5, in the code of the game).

The modulo block can be found in the "Operators" category:

The algorithm is largely unchanged, although there are a few notable differences:

1. Set the counter to zero.

2. Set the direction up.

3. Continue until the mouse is clicked:

4. Check to see whether the counter mod 5 is equal to 0:

5. If this is the case, reverse the direction.

6. Increase the current direction of the arrow by one.

7. Add one to the counter.

And the code is as follows:

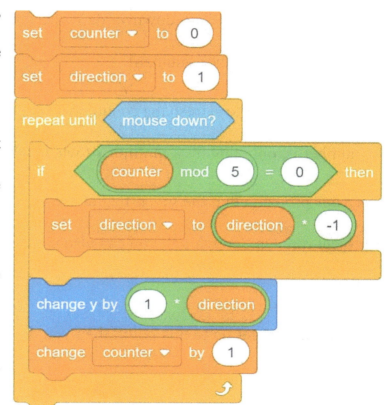

1. There are a few points to make regarding why it operates the way it does.

2. I'm keeping track of direction via a new variable named "direction," which should be either 1 or -1.

3. The "if" block's condition has been changed by "counter mod 5 = 0." When this occurs, the new direction variable is multiplied by -1, making it positive if it is negative and negative if it is positive. This occurs if the counter is a multiple of 5.

4. Because up is positive on the y-axis and down is negative on the y-axis, the block "Change y by 1 * direction" will start climbing if the direction variable is positive and downwards if the direction variable is negative, according to Scratch's standard.

5. There's no need to refresh the counter because it doesn't matter how big the number is, only that it's a multiple of what we're using in our "if" block.

To test your project, click the green flag at the top of the stage area, and watch your project run. On Scratch 3.0, you can also use the see project page to run the project.

If you were able to get up to this point, then you deserve to give yourself a high five.

Were you able to successfully recreate this project?

_____

What lessons did you learn from this project?

_____

Did you have to adjust some sections of the instruction to make it work?

If yes, what did you change or add to make this project work for you?

Practice Exercises 6

1. Make your cat ask for a number and when you enter a number, the cat should tell if the number was even or odd.

2. Make the dragon ask your name and the next time you ask the dragon what your name was, then it would tell you your name.

3. Make the ball jump exactly four times using any conditional statement(s).

Project #7: Variables and And Block

Variables in Scratch are like boxes because they are used to store values. You may use variables to assign a value to a name so that it becomes easier later on in the program to identify and refer to that value. Variables are very popular in many programming languages, in fact, without the use of variables, we would not be able to achieve a lot of things where values change on their own in the course of a program. They are used to store scores, size, player number, or whatever else you choose! To make a variable, click the "Make a Variable" button, name it, and then click "OK!" Kids should be encouraged to use variables early on and to develop and adjust variables while keeping track of what occurs.

So, in this project, Adora wants to create a Scratch project of her doll, remember Adora had a doll she called Dollie?

Yes, she wants this doll to be able to jump up and down, she also wants Dollie to get tired after jumping for a while. You do get tired sometimes after jumping around for a while, don't you? If you use the forever loop for this, Dollie will keep jumping forever and never get tired, but Adora does not want Dollie to keep jumping, she wants Dollie to stop after a while without her having to stop the program.

How do you think she will be able to achieve this? She has decided to use a variable to achieve this. Well, let us watch how Adora intends to do this. She wants to create a variable she will name, Stamina. Remember, you can give your variable any name you want, as long as it starts with an alphabet, you can even add numbers to it. So, if she wanted, Adora could have had a variable named Stamina1, Stamina1394, and so on. But for now, Adora is okay with having just one variable named Stamina1. Also note that variables are case sensitive, which means stamina is going to be different from Stamina. Very little things like these are very important in coding. Variables also can have longer names like phrases but should not have spaces like you would have in a sentence. You can use underscores to replace spaces, for example, you can have a variable with the name; new_level_1_score.

So, this is how she went about her project.

1. First, she dragged a Sprite that resembles her doll into the stage area. She decided to use the Ballerina Sprite.

Ballerina

You can try and see if Ballerina has other costumes, you now know how to check, don't you? If you don't, you can look up the previous lesson to learn how to.

2. She then added "when space key is pushed" piece from the Block Palette's Events section.

3. She clicked on Variables and selected the "Make a new variable option."

4. Like we already told you, she named the variable "Stamina", please know that you do not have to also use this name. This step will add to the list of variables and will show up under the variable category. You can check to see for yourself.

5. Then, she selected the option "this Sprite only" and choose ok.

6. She then dragged the "set (my variable) to (0)". You can now follow along from now on.

7. Now click on the "my variable option" and select Stamina or whatever name you chose as your variable name in your previous step above.

8. Change the value to 100 and click on this block to set your variable to 100.

9. From the events section, you can now drag the "When (Space) key pressed" block and couple it with "change Stamina by (0)." Change the value from 0 to -20. Remember to use the name of the variable you previously set if you are not using Stamina as your variable name.

10. From the Motion block, drag "change y by (10)" and change its value to 30. The value here determines how high Dollie is going to be able to jump.

11. From the Looks menu drag the "say (Hello) for (2) seconds" and change the variables (Hello) to (Jumping!) and 0.25 seconds. This way when Dollie is in the air, it will say "Jumping" to notify the player.

12. Add the wait block from the Control section and set the value to 0.25 so that the jump and coming down to the original position is not instant.

13. Drag the "change y by (10)" block and change the value to -30. The value entered here should be the negative of whatever value you put in the previous change y block.

14. To prevent the value from becoming a negative value, we use an If-then block where we check if Dollie's Stamina reaches 0, then Dollie stops jumping for about three seconds to catch her breath and get new stamina. To do that, add the "If-Then" block from the Control category, then from the Operator's category, drag the "< >=50" block in the open position on the "If-Then" block, change that 50 to 0 and drag the variable "Stamina" into the blank slot. You can use reference the illustration below.

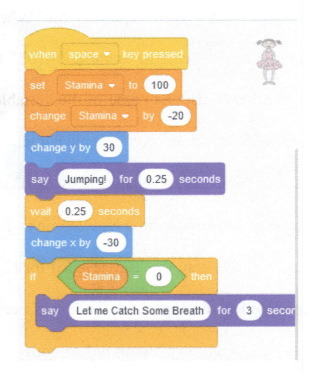

15. Now to increase the Stamina or Energy, we make another set of blocks, side by side with our previous one. For this, we use the "When (up arrow) key pressed" block.

16. Add a wait of 3 seconds so that the health does not regenerate instantly. The total wait time should exceed the total time taken by our previous set of blocks.

17. Drag the "repeat until" block from the control category.

18. As you may have probably noticed, just like the "If-Then" block, the repeat until block also has a blank space where you have to drag a block from the operator block into the slot for it. You can experiment by trying to drag a block from any other section and you will notice that only certain blocks from the operator category can fit in there.

19. Drag the "< >=50" block in the open position on the "repeat-until" block, change the 50 to 100 and drag the variable "Stamina" into the blank slot.

20. Within the "repeat-until" block, select and drag change my variable by 1 into the slot on the repeat-until block. Click the "my variable" to change it to Stamina or whatever variable name you used.

21. Change the 1 to 10. "Change Stamina by 10" increases our Dollie's Stamina, once you press the "up arrow" button, wait for 3seconds and watch how the value of the space bar will keep doing this until the value of Stamina reaches 100. Hurray, Dollie has got her full strength back and we will not have been able to do this if we did not use a variable.

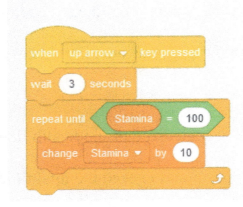

To test your project, click the green flag at the top of the stage area, press your space bar and watch your project run.

If you were able to get up to this point, then you deserve to give yourself a high five.

You may have noticed that your Sprite goes out of the screen so that it seems to be lost. We can modify the second part of our block so that pressing the "up arrow" button will not only increase the value of the stamina but will return our sprite to its previous position.

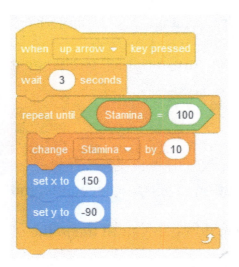

To do that, drag your Sprite to the position you want it to always start from. Note the x and y coordinates, you know how to do that, don't you? If you have forgotten, quickly refer back to project 5. Now, edit the second block of code by adding the following blocks: Set x to … and Set y to…

Once you do that, after the first set of blocks finish running and the Sprite has run out of stamina, we can then use the Up-arrow button to increase the stamina and return the sprite to its previous location so that we can keep playing around with our project.

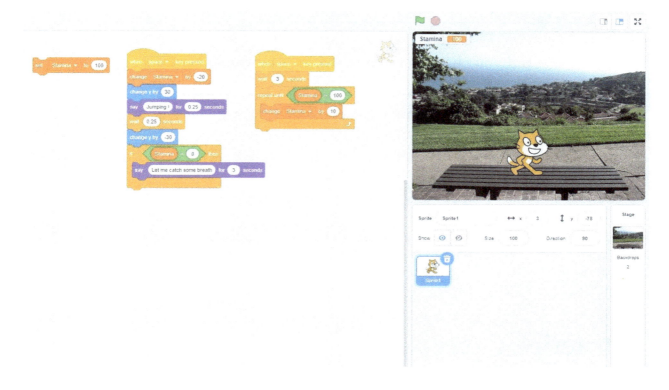

To test your project, click the green flag at the top of the stage area, and watch your project run. On Scratch 3.0, you can also use the see project page to run the project.

If you were able to get up to this point, then you deserve to give yourself a high

five.

Were you able to successfully recreate this project?

_____

What lessons did you learn from this project?

_____

Did you have to adjust some sections of the instruction to make it work?

_____

If yes, what did you change or add to make this project work for you?

Variables can also be used to keep the scores of a game and have that scores

increase when you win by using the change variable block and increasing with a

positive number whereas the number can be reduced when you lose a game. You

can end the game by saying when the variable value gets to zero, then Game Over.

Isn't it fun? I bet it is.

Practice Exercises 7

1. Create a variable and name it "Scores"

2. Switch the backdrop to Castle 3.

3. Using the variables, change the x and y position in a way that it seems your

   character is moving up on the stairs.

Project #8: Adding Sounds to Projects

Sounds (Scratch Block Category)

Sound Blocks, which are pink/magenta in hue, are used to regulate sound operations.

Here is how you can add sounds in Scratch:

1. Choose a Sprite to which you want to add a Sound.

2. Some Sprites include their own Sounds, which can get accessed by choosing the Sprite to which you want to add a Sound and then clicking the Sounds tab above the Block Palette.

3. Sounds linked with your Sprite will display in the Sound List in the Sound Editor on the left side of your screen.

4. To change the Sound, click Choose a Sound in the lower-left corner of the Sound Editor.

5. The magnifying glass icon should be selected.

6. Select the sound area.

7. It will open the Scratch Sound collection. To find a Sound, you may scroll through all Sounds, use the search box, or pick a category from the top of the menu.

8. By hovering over the play button in the upper right corner of the Soundtrack, you may try any sound.

9. By left-clicking on the Sound you want to use, you can add it. Select any sound from the menu.

10. The Sound you choose will display at the bottom of the Sound List on the left side of the Sound Editor.

If the device you're using includes a microphone for speech recording, you can also make your own Sound. To do this, you:

1. Navigate to the Sounds tab, which is located above the Block Palette.

2. Navigate to Choose a Sound in the Sound Editor's bottom left corner.

3. To record your own Sound, click the microphone button.

4. On your screen, you will see the Record Soundbox.

5. When you're ready, use the orange Record button to start recording your own Sound. When you press the Record button, the recording will begin.

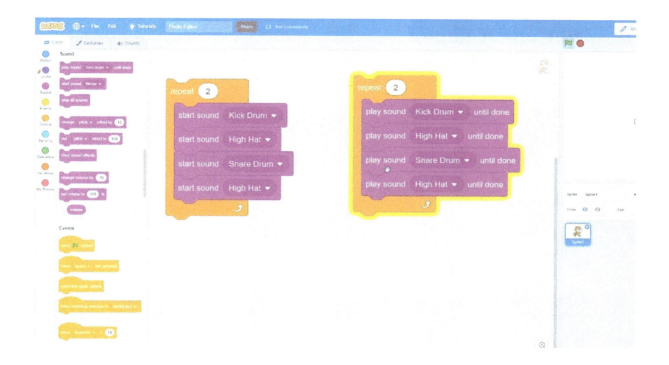

Test Your Recorded Sounds:

Select the blue Play button to listen to your recording. You may also trim the beginning and finish of your recording by dragging the orange dots to the appropriate place.

If you want to restart your recording, you can click the blue Re-record button. When you've completed your recording, click the blue Save button. Your voice recording will show at the bottom of the Sound List on the left side of the Sound Editor.

To change the name of your voice recording, click on it in the left menu. Click within the white Sound bubble to rename it by removing the existing name and typing the desired name. The name of your recording in the Sound List will be changed because of this.

How to Code A Sound

Here is how you can code a sound:

1. Drag a 'when green flag is clicked' block from the Events panel over your Code Area.

2. When the green flag appeared, I clicked the block.

3. Drag a 'play sound till end' block from the Sounds panel to your Code Area. It will activate the sound block.

4. Select the Sound you want to utilize in your code from the drop-down selection in the 'play sound till end' block. It will bring up the Play sound drop-down menu.

5. Your code will resemble the one below.

6. Stacking of code blocks

7. Put your Sound to the test. Then to execute your script, click on the Green flag above your Stage or on the 'when green flag clicked' code block in your Code Area.

Here is how you can add multiple sounds to your code:

1. Click and drag a 'wait 1 seconds' block from the Control panel onto your Code Area behind your 'play sound X till end' block. Placing a wait block

116

amongst sounds will allow you to hear each Sound clearly from start to finish. By clicking within the white bubble and inputting your desired seconds, you may adjust the duration between Sounds to make it shorter or longer.

2. Drag a new 'play sound X till the end' block out from the Sounds panel over your Code Area, next to your 'wait 1 seconds' block. Select the Sound you want to utilize in your code from the drop-down selection in the 'play sound X till end' block.

Adding multiple Sounds is a bit tricky, so you might want to test out your sounds!

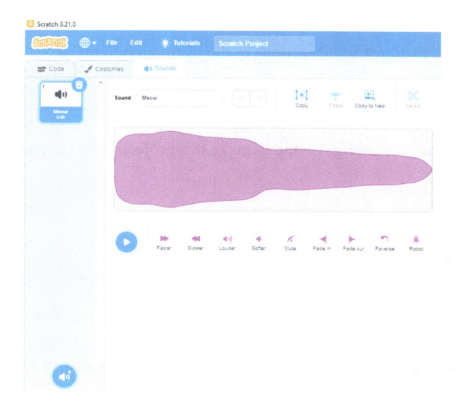

To test your project, click the green flag at the top of the stage area, and watch your project run. On Scratch 3.0, you can also use the see project page to run the project.

If you were able to get up to this point, then you deserve to give yourself a high five.

Were you able to successfully recreate this project?

_____

What lessons did you learn from this project?

_____

Did you have to adjust some sections of the instruction to make it work?

_____

If yes, what did you change or add to make this project work for you?

_____

Practice Exercises 9

1. Make all the Sprites that you made and used stand in the Concert backdrop.

2. Exactly after 0.25 seconds, their costume should change.

3. After 6 costume changes, they move to different coordinates.

4. Every Sprite should make its own sound.

5. Make a Sprite that looks like you and jumps down on the stage of the Concert.

6. Your Sprite should now sing a song. The song should be in bubbles and recorded as well.

7. After 4 lines of the song, one of your Sprite should start singing with you.

8. In the end, your Sprite should jump into the crowd.

Advanced Tips for Teachers

Tutors can help guide the kids on how to take advantage of the features that Scratch offers to be able to come up with more solutions by utilizing fewer codes. Some of the tips and notes below can help.

Use More of the Desktop Scratch for Learning

Even though Scratch doesn't allow users to share their projects directly from the desktop app, users are allowed to export their projects into the online app. This has led a lot of users to prefer the online Scratch version, since sharing projects is a lot easier with the online version because the installed desktop version does not even require users to log in or to create accounts. This supposed limitation does have a lot of advantages, especially when trying to teach kids how to use Scratch.

For example, if a teacher wants to conduct a test or wants to see how much a kid knows about Scratch then it is safer for the teacher to let them use the app. Otherwise, the student can cheat or get help if using the online Scratch 3.0.

Don't Repeat Yourself (Use Backpack)

In this brief lesson, I'll teach you how to utilize the "Backpack" feature of the Scratch online editor to transport code snippets and other items across Scratch projects.

Using the Backpack is one method for avoiding repetition as you build new and more complicated Scratch applications. Along the way, you'll learn about the computational notion of "library" and how they assist to promote the "Don't Repeat Yourself" philosophy.

The term "don't repeat yourself," short for DRY, is an implementation of the computational thinking idea of simplification, and it implies avoiding repetition in your code as much as possible. There are two ways to accomplish this with Scratch:

- Custom blocks inside a sprite are essentially a shortcut that you may utilize to decrease the number of times the same code pattern occurs.

- If you require several sprites performing essentially the same thing, you may utilize clones and costumes inside a project/sprite. It helps to avoid having duplicate sprites.

The Scratcher's difficulty, however, is to adhere to the DRY concept throughout projects. In addition to the points mentioned above, this could entail not having to re-upload the very same sprites and costumes to different projects multiple times. Moreover, you don't have to rename all the activities associated with those to what you want.

If not, then it could mean not having to individually remake blocks in a new project which you already created previously. Scratch provides "remixing" as a remedy to these problems. However, remixing entails duplicating a whole project.

What if you only wanted to duplicate a portion of a project? Or, as you gain experience, what if you wanted to merge various aspects of several projects?

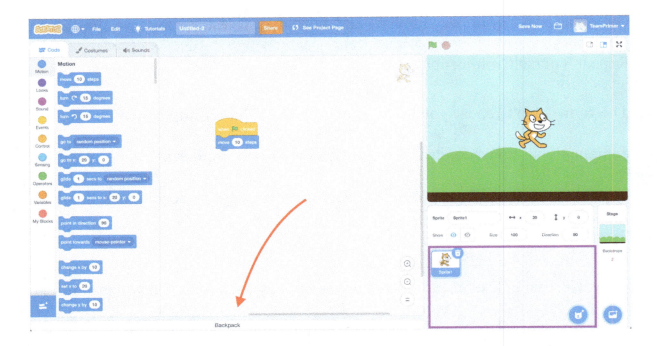

Read the code out loud

Reading over the code and tracing it on paper is a frequent debugging approach for both (children and adults). To facilitate this, it is a good practice for kids to have paper and pencil available when working. Whenever practicing with sprites in Scratch, one student can read the code while another person acts out what the Sprite does by walking around the room or sketching on paper.

Use Variables with Descriptive Names

When you begin to have many variables in your project, it may become very difficult to know what each variable is used to store when you return to that project. Imagine if someone shared a project with you that contains a lot of variables, and you are not able to identify what they stand for. Programmers tend to use implicit variable names like scores, level, stage, coordinates, size, direction, volume, tempo, instrument, pen_size, and pen_color. You will notice that these are easier to identify in the future.

Contrast Set and Adjust Blocks

Students frequently utilize set blocks to create a change block and vice versa. "Set ignores the variable's previous value," while "Change alters the old value of the variable." When the kids use the wrong blocks in their codes, it is a good practice to try to understand what they are trying to achieve by questioning them.

Questions like, "Are you trying to set the variable or to modify the variable value?" and "What's the difference between set and change?"

There is a key difference between set and change.

- **Set**: The block will change the value to what you input here.
- **Change**: The block will add or subtract the value you input to/from the previous value.

Example of Set Block: If in my Spiderman platformer game, you lose three health then I would want you to restart the level. For this, I will set the value of X to the start position, irrespective of what your current position is.

Example of Change Block: If Superman flies to the top of a building then Batman has to use an elevator. Now I give you the option to choose any of the two elevators, and here I will use the change block to change the y position of the elevator and Batman.

Make Use of "& wait" Blocks

When students utilize numerous play-sound blocks in a sequence, they may become confused because if the play-sound-until-done blocks are not used, the sounds begin in rapid succession before the preceding sound has finished playing. Students may also become perplexed when sending messages due to the distinction between broadcast blocks and broadcast-and-wait blocks. I propose that students use "until done" or "and wait" to ensure that their code blocks execute consecutively.

And Wait is one of the lines available in multiple blocks like Broadcast and wait, ask, and wait, and play sound until done. Wait until a separate block puts a halt to everything until the condition is met. These are important, otherwise, all your plans will be jumbled.

A simple scenario to explain the significance of this is:

If a cat and dog are talking with each other and I only use the play sound option, then both the cat and dog will be speaking at the same time which creates a mess. If I use the play sound until done option, then the next thing will happen after the sound has ended. It means when the cat has meowed and asked the dog his name, then the dog will answer. Both things will not happen at the same time, which

improves our animation

Last Words

We hope that you can use this guide to make great projects and share them with us. Do keep in mind that Scratch has similar elements with other coding languages like C++, phyton, and the likes, but instead of typing you simply use blocks to achieve these things. Coding with Scratch will most definitely take you to places and help you in your future ventures, all the while having fun!

www.ingramcontent.com/pod-product-compliance
Lightning Source LLC
Chambersburg PA
CBHW081228050326
40690CB00013B/2695